Sotto Voce

Books by Nilo Cruz available from TCG

Anna in the Tropics

Ana en el Trópico

Beauty of the Father

The Color of Desire / Hurricane

Sotto Voce

Two Sisters and a Piano and Other Plays
ALSO INCLUDES:
A Bicycle Country
Capricho
Hortensia and the Museum of Dreams
Lorca in a Green Dress

Sotto Voce

◄o►

Nilo Cruz

THEATRE COMMUNICATIONS GROUP   NEW YORK   2016

Sotto Voce is published by Theatre Communications Group, Inc.,
520 Eighth Avenue, 24th Floor, New York, NY 10018-4156

The epigraph on page ix is from *Destiny and Desire* by Carlos Fuentes, published in 2011 by Random House Publishing Group.

The publication of *Sotto Voce* by Nilo Cruz, through TCG's Book Program, is made possible in part by the New York State Council on the Arts with the support of Governor Andrew Cuomo and the New York State Legislature.

TCG books are exclusively distributed to the book trade by Consortium Book Sales and Distribution.

LIBRARY OF CONGRESS CATALOGING-IN-PUBLICATION DATA

Cruz, Nilo, author.
Sotto voce / by Nilo Cruz.
ISBN 9781559365062 (trade paper)
ISBN 9781559368346 (ebook)
DDC 812/.6—dc23

Cover design, book design and composition by Lisa Govan
Cover art by Fernando Teijeiro
Author photo by Todd Rosenberg

First Edition, May 2016

For Natasha Parry
and Peter Brook

———◄o►———

Acknowledgments

————◄○►————

The author would like to thank Franca Sofia Barchiesi
for making useful comments when the play was
in preparation for production.

If the sea were to shout,
we would all be deaf.

—Carlos Fuentes,
Destiny and Desire

Sotto Voce

Production History

Sotto Voce received its world premiere at Theatre for the New City (Crystal Field, Artistic Director) in New York on February 15, 2014. It was directed by Nilo Cruz. The scenic design was by Adrian W. Jones, the lighting design was by Alexander Bartenieff, the sound design and original music were by Erik T. Lawson and the costume design was by Anita Yavich; the production stage manager was Charles Casano.

BEMADETTE KAHN	Franca Sofia Barchiesi
SAQUIEL RAFAELI	Andhy Mendez
LUCILA PULPO	Arielle Jacobs

CHARACTERS

BEMADETTE KAHN: An eighty-year-old woman who has aged gracefully; time has been good to her and she looks more like she's in her sixties

SAQUIEL RAFAELI: A twenty-eight-year-old man of Jewish-Cuban descent; he is passionate and romantic; he has worked hard at creating a unique and bohemian look for himself

LUCILA PULPO: A woman in her thirties; although she appears to be tough, it is all a veneer to protect her fragile soul

NINA STRAUSS: A woman in her twenties, played by the actor playing Lucila

ARIEL STRAUSS: A man in his twenties, played by the actor playing Saquiel

TIME AND PLACE

The millennium. New York City.

Set

Bernadette's apartment. There is a large white curtain on which images of the sea are projected. Downstage from the curtain there is a large table full of books, a modern telephone, and intriguing objects that provide inspiration for Ms. Kahn. There are three chairs, one behind the table and two at each end. Further down, stage left, there's an art deco armchair.

Author's Note

When the characters write emails, no computers are used, only sounds to illustrate how technology is used as a means of communication.

Act One

As the lights begin to dim, we hear the cries of seagulls and the constant sound of a ship's horn in a harbor. Then, in full darkness, we hear the sound of someone writing on a computer keyboard and the amplified recorded voice of a woman. The sounds become an echo.

Projected on the curtain is an image of the ocean.

BEMADETTE *(Recorded voice)*: Ariel and Nina Strauss boarded the *St. Louis* ship, Saturday, May 13, 1939. They had left Hamburg with thoughts of starting a new life away from Germany and finding a new home in Havana.

(The lights reveal Bemadette.)

(Spoken voice) I wanted to be on the ship with them, but I clenched my toes inside my shoes to keep from running up the gangway, as I stood immobile on the dock,

drenched in my coat with the desire to leave with Ariel, while the air around me became still.

(A phone rings. The lights reveal Saquiel, a young man dressed in a leather coat. Bemadette picks up the phone without speaking.)

SAQUIEL: Hello? Bemadette?

(No answer from Bemadette.)

Are you there?

BEMADETTE: Yes.

SAQUIEL: It's me. Saquiel.

BEMADETTE: No, you're not Saquiel. That's not the name I gave you. You're Ariel Strauss.

SAQUIEL: I'm leaving—

BEMADETTE: Do you have to remind me?

SAQUIEL: No. But from the beginning I told you my visit would be short.

BEMADETTE: Yes. It isn't the first time you tell me this.

SAQUIEL: But you never believed me—

BEMADETTE: No. I thought I had dreamt it.

SAQUIEL: My visa expired—

BEMADETTE *(Playfully)*: My dear young man, you could have lied to me—

SAQUIEL: Lied—?

BEMADETTE: Yes.

SAQUIEL: How?

BEMADETTE: By easing the moment.

SAQUIEL: Is that what you want me to do?

BEMADETTE: I thought you would know by now—

SAQUIEL: Know what—?

BEMADETTE: To lie to me.

SAQUIEL: If I knew how to lie to you I would.

BEMADETTE: It would help me forget that you're leaving.

SAQUIEL: I think it's too late now.

BEMADETTE: It's never too late. Something is always beginning.

SAQUIEL: What could begin now?

BEMADETTE: What we have to say to each other one last time.

SAQUIEL: The sound of good-bye?

BEMADETTE: That's also a beginning. You mustn't forget to take a look at Central Park one last time.

SAQUIEL: With you?

BEMADETTE: No, by yourself. I'm not leaving. I don't need to see it one last time.

SAQUIEL: I only know how to go there with you.

BEMADETTE *(Her expression is childlike)*: In the end there's nothing to it. We only have to close our eyes and enter Central Park.

SAQUIEL: Were my eyes to close now, I'd be waiting for you there.

BEMADETTE: In what part of the park?

SAQUIEL: Where I always like to sit.

BEMADETTE: By the statue of the Cuban poet, José Martí.

SAQUIEL: And we'd visit the park with the specter of the poet.

BEMADETTE: The three of us like ghosts.

SAQUIEL: Yes. And he'd show us the trees he used to know in the park.

BEMADETTE: The last trees to drop their leaves in the fall.

SAQUIEL: And the ones to bloom first . . .

BEMADETTE: Of course, he would've known all the trees.

SAQUIEL: And so did Walt Whitman . . .

BEMADETTE: And Edith Wharton . . .

SAQUIEL: Bemadette, I must go. I have to go.

BEMADETTE *(Suddenly, desperately but quietly)*: Don't go yet! Don't go, Saquiel!

SAQUIEL: Do you realize that if I don't leave I might not be allowed to come back?

(She doesn't respond.)

Bemadette. Are you there? Would you read my letters when I write to you?

BEMADETTE: I'd much rather hear your voice—
SAQUIEL: That's not what I asked you—
BEMADETTE: I know—
SAQUIEL: Good-bye then—

(Sound of a dial tone. Bemadette is unable to end the phone call. The lights go down on Saquiel.)

BEMADETTE: How did I spend these same hours the past years without his voice?
How did I get myself into this? How did it begin?

(Lights change. Bemadette takes us back to the initial conversation that occurred a month ago with Saquiel.
The telephone rings. The answering machine picks up the call. Lights up on Saquiel.)

SAQUIEL: Ms. Kahn . . . Ms. Kahn . . . it's me, Saquiel, the student from Cuba. Don't hang up. It doesn't matter if you don't talk to me. You don't have to tell me a word. I want to tell you why I've come to see you. —Ms. Kahn, are you there?

(Not a word from her.)

I couldn't keep from doing it. Are you listening to me?

(Not a word from her.)

After months of organizing letters for a group of *St. Louis* passengers . . . maybe you know of them. Do you, Ms. Kahn?

(Not a word from her.)

—Ms. Kahn, it's all right . . . it's all right if you don't respond. After months of gathering letters . . . months of organizing records and lists of Jewish passengers who traveled on the *St. Louis* ship, I came upon your letters . . . Do you remember the love letters you sent to Ariel Strauss, the young man from Berlin, who was traveling on that ship?

(Sound of a beep, indicating that Bernadette has picked up the receiver and is now on the phone with him.)

BERNADETTE: What about Ariel Strauss?

SAQUIEL: Good, Ms. Kahn, I finally hear your voice.

BERNADETTE: Yes, I was listening to your message.

SAQUIEL: I'm glad you decided to speak to me.

BERNADETTE: Yes, go on.

SAQUIEL: Well, as I said, I have the letters you sent to him.

BERNADETTE: Then send them to me.

SAQUIEL: I don't have them with me. They're back in Cuba.

BERNADETTE: Then why are you calling me?

SAQUIEL: Do you know of a small group of former *St. Louis* passengers?

BERNADETTE: No. I don't know anything about it.

SAQUIEL: They want to hold a reunion in Miami.

BERNADETTE: What kind of reunion?

SAQUIEL: Similar to the one held back in 1989 to commemorate the fiftieth anniversary of the sailing of the *St. Louis* ship.

BERNADETTE: But I wasn't a former passenger on that ship.

SAQUIEL: Yes, I know. You're not even Jewish.

BERNADETTE: What about Ariel Strauss? Why did you mention him?

SAQUIEL: I thought it was important to contact you. We're interested in the stories of the missing passengers and I thought you could help us.

BEMADETTE: I lost track of Ariel Strauss.

SAQUIEL: I understand . . .

BEMADETTE: I'm sorry I can't help you—

SAQUIEL: Please don't hang up! Maybe you can tell us a little of his background.

BEMADETTE: And what good would this do?

SAQUIEL: What we want is a human story of a tragedy that was forgotten.

BEMADETTE: It's a little too late. I'm sorry. I can't help you.

SAQUIEL: Don't hang up. We think that the United States and Cuba should apologize.

BEMADETTE: Apologize for what?

SAQUIEL: For turning away a German ship carrying 937 Jewish refugees.

BEMADETTE: Sorry, I can't help you.

SAQUIEL: Don't you think it's about time for an apology?

BEMADETTE: Is that why you're calling me?

SAQUIEL: Yes, but also for more personal and selfish reasons . . .

BEMADETTE: Such as?

SAQUIEL: My being a writer . . .

BEMADETTE: Oh no!

SAQUIEL: I . . . I also wanted to meet you.

BEMADETTE: Impossible.

SAQUIEL: Ms. Kahn, please don't hang up.

BEMADETTE: Young man, for many years I've tried to forget what happened with the *St. Louis.*

I can't help you.

(Bemadette hangs up the phone.)

SAQUIEL: Ms. Kahn . . . Ms. Kahn . . .

(Bernadette walks to another part of the room, lost in thought. The phone rings. Lucila, the house cleaner, enters.)

LUCILA: Should I answer the phone?

BERNADETTE: No.

LUCILA: Whoever is calling is very persistent.

BERNADETTE: It's probably the young student.

(The phone stops ringing. Lights fade down on Saquiel.)

LUCILA: Why did you give him your number?

BERNADETTE: I didn't.

LUCILA: How did he get it?

BERNADETTE: He must've found a way of getting it through someone . . .

LUCILA: I'll be damned, or he found it in the white pages.

BERNADETTE: Yes, a sly fox he's turned out to be.

LUCILA: So what are you going to do if you're not going to answer his calls?

BERNADETTE: Let him call as much as he wants until he gets tired.

LUCILA: Well, that's a way to leave him hanging.

BERNADETTE: He's crossing the line.

LUCILA: Did you draw the line in the first place?

BERNADETTE: I certainly did.

LUCILA: Did you allow him to cross it?

BERNADETTE: No.

LUCILA: Did you let the line become faint?

BERNADETTE: What's with the line!

LUCILA: Well, if you let the line become invisible and you didn't draw a new line, he's liable to do as he wills and jump into your life like a kangaroo.

BERNADETTE: Never mind "lines"! It's this whole new generation of students. For them, our work is not enough. They love to deconstruct everything we've written. They try to find hidden meaning behind every sentence and word. And the writing is never enough. They want to ask questions, they want photographs, autographs, even the dust from under our shoes. I mean, do they actually think that by talking to us we're going to disclose a secret?

LUCILA: Ay, Ms. Kahn, I don't know . . .

(Lucila exits. Saquiel appears, bathed in a pool of light. We hear the chiming sound of a computer, announcing the arrival of a new email. He looks into the distance as he speaks the words he's writing, but no keyboard is used.)

SAQUIEL: Dear Writer, are you there? Send. Dear Writer, why don't you answer? Send. Dear Writer, I'm at the library where I write to you every day. Send.

(Bernadette, also bathed in light, responds to his email. She also speaks the words she writes as she looks into the distance.)

BERNADETTE: Dear Student, you don't write to me. You write to all the characters that live in my books. Send.

SAQUIEL: Dear Writer, that's because you are Guilaine, Vera, Nadine . . . Send.

BERNADETTE: You are mistaken, dear Student. Those are names I invented, names I filled with words and memories, names that I assigned faces and bodies to . . . Send.

SAQUIEL: Why won't you let me meet you in person and interview you? Send.

BERNADETTE: My dear student, be understanding. Who you might want to meet no longer exists. You can meet me in my books. Send.

SAQUIEL: Allow me to see you just once. Just once. I have discovered where you live. Let me visit you. Send.

BEMADETTE: Dear Student, don't waste your time. Why would I interrupt my solitude, if I haven't let anybody into my life in many years? Delete.

SAQUIEL: Are you still there, Writer? Send. Hello! Send. Answer me. Hello. Answer me, please! Send.

BEMADETTE: My dear student, I don't let myself be seen. I don't go out. Why would I let myself be taken by the external agitations of your studies? My life as a writer has provided me with my own desolation and consolation. Send.

SAQUIEL: I will be discreet as the quiet that inhabits your walls. Send.

(Lucila enters. Lights down on Saquiel.)

LUCILA: Was that the student again?

BEMADETTE: Who else?

LUCILA: You were happy when he started sending you letters.

BEMADETTE: Yes. I found them amusing and quite touching.

LUCILA: You were fine when he started sending you emails.

BEMADETTE *(Snaps)*: What are you trying to get at? He's stalking me. Have you ever been stalked?

LUCILA: Many times.

BEMADETTE *(Knowing she's lying)*: Really?

LUCILA: You think you're the only one who's important?

BEMADETTE: I don't think anything.

LUCILA: Then we both know what it's like.

BEMADETTE: What is it like, Lucila?

LUCILA: Stalking? A stalker?

BEMADETTE: Uh-huh . . .

LUCILA: How do you say it . . . ? A stalker is someone . . .

BEMADETTE: Someone . . .

LUCILA: I don't know . . . someone who . . .

BEMADETTE: Yes, someone . . .

LUCILA: . . . who lives in the dark. *(Nicely put)* And he's obsessed with stealing other people's light.
BEMADETTE: Is that a stalker to you?
LUCILA: I don't think he means any harm.

(The computer chimes.)

You got more mail.
BEMADETTE: I heard.
LUCILA: Aren't you going to respond?
BEMADETTE: Don't you have work to do?

(Lucila exits. Lights reveal Saquiel.)

SAQUIEL: Dear Writer, I don't have much time left in this country. Have you changed your mind? Send.
BEMADETTE: Dear Student, do not insist. For many years I have succumbed to the refuge of these walls, the security of a lock and the obedience of a doorman who guards my solitude. And I'd like my seclusion to be undisturbed. Send.
SAQUIEL: Then let me call you again. Send. Let me hear your voice. Send.
BEMADETTE: But it's better if I write to you. My voice is old and cracked, unlike the voice of Vera and Nadine and the rest of the women who inhabit my books. Send.
SAQUIEL: It's the voice of those names and that's enough for me . . . Send. Please, accept my phone call. Send. I'm interested in knowing more about Ariel Strauss, the young man from Berlin. Send.

(A moment. Reflection.)

BEMADETTE: Be patient with all the questions you might have about people I mentioned in my books. Let the questions

14

live in you, in the same way I let my books live and take their own course in life. Let the questions mature in your being, then one day you'll discover the answers before you. Send.

SAQUIEL: Are you still there? Send. Are you still there? Send. Writer? Send. Answer me, please. Send.

(Lights down on Saquiel. The phone rings. Lucila enters.)

BEMADETTE: Don't answer. It could be the student.
LUCILA: It could be the doorman.
BEMADETTE: I'm not expecting anyone.
LUCILA: It could be the superintendent.
BEMADETTE: He would ring the bell.
LUCILA: I ordered a pizza.
BEMADETTE: Then go downstairs and get it.
LUCILA: I was hoping this young student would become your friend and . . .

(Bemadette gives her a look.)

BEMADETTE: *Und was?* [And what?]
LUCILA: I don't know . . . that he'd get you out of the house and . . .
BEMADETTE: *Und?* [And?]
LUCILA: Just for a change of pace. Look at me . . . I'm starting to have a new life. My husband was a bore like . . . like . . .
BEMADETTE: Like me . . . you can say it . . .
LUCILA: Oh, I wasn't going to say that, Ms. Kahn.
BEMADETTE: It's all right. I'm not offended. I know I suffer from agoraphobia. I admit it.
LUCILA: What is that, Ms. Kahn?
BEMADETTE: Someone who doesn't like leaving the house.

LUCILA: Ah! Like an Angora cat. My husband was like one of those cats, furry and housebound. He had hairs in places where I never thought hair could grow.

BEMADETTE: *Ach, nein!* [Oh, no.]

LUCILA: Well, it's true. Never thought I liked a hairy back. But making love to him was like petting a panther or a bear.

BEMADETTE: *Wie unangenehm!* [How unpleasant!]

LUCILA: Ay, I'm sorry, Ms. Kahn. You don't need to know these things.

BEMADETTE: No, that's all right, darling, if you enjoy a furry back . . . I myself have always preferred a less-forested man.

(They both laugh.)

LUCILA: Ay, Ms. Kahn, it was very sad my husband's case. That was the part that did us in . . .

BEMADETTE: His hairy back?

(More laughter from the two of them.)

LUCILA: No, not going out anywhere. *(Making her point now)* I love to go out. I love the nightlife. After a couple of years of being married our outings consisted of pretending to go out.

BEMADETTE: Having dates at home you mean?

LUCILA: Sure, all it would take were two pounds of pork loin and I'd land him in Colombia through a delicious stew of pork and cassava. And with a leg of lamb with mint and couscous I'd take him as far as Morocco.

BEMADETTE: That far?

LUCILA: Ah, that's nothing! Through a dish of curry prawns with coconut milk, I'd take him straight to Bali.

BEMADETTE: I didn't know you were an international chef.

LUCILA: Ay, no, Ms. Kahn! I was more like a doomed flight attendant, twenty pounds overweight from all the cooking. Because in the end, the only place the meals took us were to city hall for a divorce.

(The phone rings.)

BEMADETTE: *Was ist das? Schon wieder! . . . Gott, hilf mir! Nein, Ich kann nicht mehr!* [What is this? Again? God help me! No, I can't take this anymore!]

(Frustrated, Bemadette goes out. Lucila answers the phone.)

LUCILA: Hello, Ms. Kahn's residence.

(Lights up on Saquiel, holding a bouquet of flowers.)

SAQUIEL: Bemadette.
LUCILA: Hold one moment please. *(In a loud voice to Bemadette)* It's the student.
BEMADETTE *(Offstage)*: He shouldn't be calling me. Tell him I'm not at home.
LUCILA *(To Saquiel)*: Hold on. *(To Bemadette)* He probably knows you're always here.

(Bemadette reenters.)

BEMADETTE: Tell him I'm ill.
LUCILA *(To Saquiel)*: Ms. Kahn is sick.
SAQUIEL: Oh, that's a shame.
LUCILA *(To Saquiel)*: May I ask who's calling?
SAQUIEL: Saquiel.
LUCILA *(With sensuality)*: Hello, Saquiel.

(Bemadette rolls her eyes.)

I help her with the housecleaning. My name is Lucila.

SAQUIEL: Will I be able to visit her?

LUCILA *(To Saquiel)*: Where are you calling from?

BEMADETTE: Hang up.

SAQUIEL: I'm across the street.

LUCILA *(To Bemadette)*: He says he's standing across the street.

BEMADETTE: How dare him! Tell him I'm going to call the police.

LUCILA *(To Saquiel)*: She says she's in bed.

BEMADETTE: *Was?!* [What?!]

LUCILA *(To Saquiel)*: I mean, Ms. Kahn . . . she's in bed.

SAQUIEL: I can see the light from her room.

LUCILA *(To Bemadette)*: He says he can see the light from your room.

BEMADETTE: Unbelievable! Hang up!

LUCILA *(To Saquiel, dismissing what Bemadette said)*: That's because I'm cleaning. I'm cleaning.

BEMADETTE: What are you doing? Hang up!

SAQUIEL: I brought her some flowers.

LUCILA *(To Saquiel)*: You did?

SAQUIEL: Should I leave them with the doorman?

BEMADETTE: What is he saying?

SAQUIEL: I brought her flowers. I'll leave them with the doorman. Tell her that I sent them to her.

LUCILA *(To Saquiel)*: Uh-hum . . . from you to her. Yes. Uh-hum . . .

BEMADETTE: Give me the phone.

LUCILA *(To Bemadette in one breath, speaking rapidly from excitement)*: He said he brought you some flowers. He's going to give them to the doorman so the doorman can give them to the elevator man and the elevator man can give them to me so I can give them to you.

BEMADETTE: Tell him thank you, good-bye and hang up.

LUCILA: Ay, Bemadette!

BEMADETTE: Tell him.

SAQUIEL: Are you still there?

LUCILA *(To Saquiel)*: So we want to thank you . . .

SAQUIEL: Yes . . .

BEMADETTE: Not we. The flowers are not for you.

SAQUIEL: What did you say?

BEMADETTE: Hang up!

LUCILA *(To Saquiel)*: So thank you, good-bye and I'll hang up now. Ms. Kahn will call you tomorrow.

BEMADETTE: I will do no such a thing!

LUCILA *(To Saquiel)*: No, you call her tomorrow.

BEMADETTE: Don't tell him that!

LUCILA *(To Saquiel)*: So thank you again. I'll hang up now. Good-bye. Ciao.

(Lucila hangs up the phone. Lights down on Saquiel.)

BEMADETTE: What's gotten into you?

LUCILA: Ms. Kahn, you just got flowers.

BEMADETTE: I don't care about any flowers.

LUCILA: Let's look out the window to see what he looks like.

(She turns off the lights and runs to the window.)

BEMADETTE: Absolutely not. You're acting like a fifteen year old.

LUCILA *(Looking out)*: Ay, Ms. Kahn, he's a peach.

BEMADETTE: Get away from that window. We've lost a lot of time in useless chatter.

LUCILA: I'll go downstairs and get the flowers.

BEMADETTE: No, you will not. I mean really . . . ! Will you stop this nonsense!

LUCILA: It's time for me to go. I'll go get my purse.

(She exits to get her purse.)

BEMADETTE: No. You're not leaving now.

(Lucila reenters with her purse.)

LUCILA: Don't worry! I won't steal him from you.

BEMADETTE: You talk so foolishly sometimes.

LUCILA: It's true. Remember I'm myopic. If I don't wear my glasses, I won't see him when I go out. *(Takes off her glasses)* See right there, where you're standing . . . it's all a haze.

BEMADETTE: Honestly, Lucila!

(Lucila puts her glasses back on. She takes out a powder compact and starts powdering her face.)

LUCILA: Myopia is not a handicap, Ms. Kahn. You just have to use it to your advantage. When I take Ms. Brookner to the fancy stores, I take off my glasses so I'm not tempted to buy anything. —And when it comes to men . . . The other night when my friend Benita Santos invited me to go dancing, I said to myself, I'm not going to wear my glasses or my contact lenses. Tonight I'm going to be myopic.

(She takes out a crayon and colors her lips.)

If a man comes and asks me to dance, I'm not going to tell him no because his nose is too big or I don't like his mustache. I'm simply going to say yes and enjoy myself dancing. And I did. I had the time of my life. —Let me get my coat.

(Lucila exits to get her coat. Bemadette approaches the window and looks out. Lucila reenters and catches Bemadette looking out the window.)

BEMADETTE: You do realize how idiotic this whole thing is.

LUCILA: Is he gone?

BEMADETTE: No.

(Lucila walks to the door.)

LUCILA: I can't stay here the whole night.

BEMADETTE: He's still standing there. You can't go just yet.

LUCILA: I'll be myopic if I see him.

BEMADETTE: *Ach mein Gott!!* [Oh my God.]

(Lucila opens the door and goes out. Bemadette goes to the window. Lights up on Saquiel. Outside, Lucila approaches Saquiel. Lights fade on Bemadette.)

LUCILA: What are you doing standing there?

SAQUIEL: Are you the owner of the sidewalk?

LUCILA: No, simply walking out the door, hurrying along . . .

SAQUIEL: If you were hurrying along, how come you noticed me?

LUCILA: Because you just happened to be standing there staring at that window.

SAQUIEL: I saw you last night when you went out of that same exact building.

LUCILA: Did you follow me?

SAQUIEL: Yes.

LUCILA: Did you enjoy following me? Should I be afraid of you and call the police? Are you a stalker?

SAQUIEL *(To himself)*: You've got to be kidding me. *(To Lucila, in a playful and exaggerated manner)* Yes, I've been following you for weeks. I have no way of stopping myself from following you. I'm Saquiel Rafaeli.

LUCILA: I'm Bemadette Kahn.

SAQUIEL: No you're not.

LUCILA: Are you here to kill her or me?

SAQUIEL: Not interested in blood.

21

LUCILA *(All in one breath)*: Good. Now let's get down to business. I just spoke to you on the phone. You're the student, she's Bemadette Kahn, I'm Lucila Pulpo, I work for her, I'm her personal assistant, her caretaker, her maid, her friend, and sometimes her cook and her security guard. I tried to help you out today, but I didn't get anywhere with her. So let me tell you something: she won't come down to meet you, so you're wasting your time.

SAQUIEL: All right.

LUCILA: And don't expect her to thank you for the flowers—

SAQUIEL: All right—

LUCILA: And much less to send you a note with the doorman or me—

SAQUIEL: Okay—

LUCILA: So give it up!

SAQUIEL: *Oyéee!* [Ouch!]

LUCILA: Go home. You won't get anywhere with her.

SAQUIEL: Woosh! You just broke my heart.

LUCILA: Then deal or go to a heart surgeon.

(She turns to leave.)

SAQUIEL: Can you help me?

(She turns to him. A moment.)

LUCILA: Just beat it, kid!

SAQUIEL: Help me out. Please. Help me connect with Ms. Kahn.

LUCILA: I already told you.

SAQUIEL: Can you help me get some information?

LUCILA: You're not asking me to be a spy, are you? An informer?

SAQUIEL: I just want to meet Ms. Kahn. What if I . . . ?

LUCILA: There're no ifs. I know so. Been working for the woman for ten years now.

SAQUIEL: But there are things I'd like to ask her.

LUCILA: Like what?

SAQUIEL *(Becoming nervous)*: Things I'd like to ask her in person . . . questions related to her life, her work . . .

LUCILA: What was your name again?

SAQUIEL: Saquiel. Saquiel Rafaeli.

LUCILA: What kind of name is that?

SAQUIEL: Saquiel means "the angel of water."

LUCILA: What kind of water? And what kind of angel?

SAQUIEL: I don't know. Just a name.

(He looks at her straight in the eyes.)

I'm just Saquiel. You?

LUCILA: Lucila Pulpo. Seriously, what are you after with Ms. Kahn?

SAQUIEL: There's certain information I need. I'm here doing research.

LUCILA: Are you a writer too?

SAQUIEL: Yes I am.

LUCILA: You got anything published?

SAQUIEL: No.

LUCILA: Then you're not a writer according to Ms. Kahn.

SAQUIEL: All right, I'm not a writer then. *(Straight into her eyes)* You're going to help me, right?

LUCILA *(Looking into his eyes)*: Leave. Don't make things difficult for me.

SAQUIEL: I've come too far to leave now.

LUCILA: What do you call far?

SAQUIEL: All I had to go through to get here.

LUCILA: That's not far in the world of Ms. Kahn. Many others have come from faraway looking for her.

SAQUIEL: And she didn't let them in.

LUCILA: Unh-unh.

SAQUIEL: Then I'll be the lucky one. I'm staying with someone who gives dancing lessons. Do you want to take a dance class with me?

LUCILA: No.

SAQUIEL: Don't you know how to dance?

LUCILA: Are you kidding me? You're talking to a Colombian from Cartagena.

SAQUIEL: And you're talking to a Jew from Cuba. The classes require a dance partner. Here's a flier with the address. They start at seven o'clock. Wear dance shoes. And don't be late. Tell them at the door you're a friend of Saquiel Rafaeli. I'll see you there.

(He turns and goes off. Lucila exits. Bemadette enters with flowers. We hear the beep of the answering machine. She listens to the message attentively.)

(Recorded voice) Bemadette. Bemadette. I know you're listening to me, I can hear you breathing. No one knows what it's like to look for someone, that is, if you've never gone out of your way to search for another person. It takes dedication and determination. Sometimes it feels as if I had nothing else to do in life but find you. I hope to meet you.

(Bemadette takes the initiative to write to Saquiel.)

BEMADETTE: Dear Student, are you at the library? Send.

(The computer chimes. The lights reveal Saquiel.)

SAQUIEL: Dear Writer. Yes I am. Send.

BEMADETTE: Dear Student, good! So, you must read my novels in a particular order: *The Scent of Wood, Gentle Rain, Immutable Time, Unguided War, Vanquished Summer* and *That Man Over There.* Send. Please don't ask me how

24

they are connected and how they got written. All I know is they took form in the malleability of time. Send.

SAQUIEL: I'm learning not to ask too many questions about your novels. Send. Did you like my flowers? Send.

BEMADETTE: They're lovely. Send.

SAQUIEL: I'm glad. Send.

BEMADETTE: I was thinking of their color, of the victory of their presence over every other color in my house. Send.

SAQUIEL: When can I see you? Send.

BEMADETTE: That won't be possible. Send.

SAQUIEL: Then let me describe myself. I always dress in black clothes. People think I'm always in mourning. In Cuba, people think I'm in a rock band, which I'm not. Women think I'm a musician who is in love with his own self because I wear kohl under my eyes. Men think I'm peculiar or gay because I'm not a sports fan. What would you think of me? Send.

BEMADETTE *(Laughs)*: That you're eccentric like me. Send.

SAQUIEL: Laughter. Send.

BEMADETTE: Writers can be unusual creatures. Send.

SAQUIEL: I'm here on a student visa. I pretty much ran out of money so I found a job walking dogs. They're my only friends in New York. Do you have a dog? Send.

BEMADETTE: No. No dogs. Only a blue parakeet. Send.

SAQUIEL: In Havana, I live in my grandfather's apartment. Send. I sleep in what used to be his bed. Send. As the light in his eyes began to fade and his German accent became thicker, he filled his room with pictures of his sister and newspaper clippings of the doomed *St. Louis* voyage. Send. This is why I am reaching out to you. Among the refugees that were denied entry into Cuba and the United States was his sister, Eleanor Rafaeli. It was my grandfather's wish for her not to be banished from history. And I've taken it upon myself to rescue my grandfather's wish. Send.

BEMADETTE: Call me on the phone. Call me now. All of a sudden I feel like listening to your voice. Send.

(The phone begins to ring. She hesitates before answering.)

SAQUIEL: Hello. Bemadette. Bemadette. Bemadette.

(Bemadette hangs up. Dial tone. Saquiel is disconcerted. Lucila comes in with a coffee tray. She begins to pour coffee for Bemadette. Lights down on Saquiel.)

BEMADETTE: You spoke to him yesterday.

LUCILA: Who?

BEMADETTE: The student. I saw you from the window.

LUCILA: Yes, he approached me when I was leaving the building.

BEMADETTE: What did he have to say?

LUCILA: What you already know, that he wants to meet you.

BEMADETTE: You talked to him for a long time.

LUCILA: I listened.

BEMADETTE: Did he have much to say?

LUCILA: My! Have you had a change of heart?

BEMADETTE: No, not at all. I'm just posing a question.

LUCILA: One of these days I'm going to sit and try to figure you out, Ms. Kahn.

BEMADETTE: You haven't answered my question.

LUCILA: I think there's something broken about him.

BEMADETTE: Well, it's not normal for a young man to stand across the street, in front of a window for hours.

LUCILA: And who wants to be normal? You're not normal.

BEMADETTE: Ah, now we're getting somewhere. It seems like you've taken an interest in the young man.

LUCILA: No.

BEMADETTE: Look at you . . . you're even blushing.

LUCILA: So what do you want me to tell you, Ms. Kahn, that I had dinner with him . . . ? And he slumped over his meat and potatoes thinking of you? And he sipped indifferently at his martini, and when I tried talking to him, he seemed not even to hear me because he was thinking of you?

BEMADETTE: My! We are feisty today!

LUCILA: Are you going to have coffee?

BEMADETTE: I don't like your tone, Lucila. You have a problem with manners. This whole country does.

LUCILA: You don't have to blame the whole country, Ms. Kahn. You can blame me.

BEMADETTE: No, I am convinced that it is a cultural collapse. And what causes this crudeness is a sort of anarchy in which everyone has lost sight of indiscretion.

LUCILA: And how can we gain back our discretion, Ms. Kahn?

BEMADETTE: Maybe through a little fear. But nowadays I don't know anymore. Nowadays no one is afraid of anything. We have lost our fear.

LUCILA: What kind of fear are you talking about?

BEMADETTE: Fear that everything will fall into a state of disorder and ruin. In the old days we used fear as a way of bettering ourselves. Wars used to remind us of our own demise.

LUCILA: I have my own fears, Ms. Kahn. Fear of invisibility . . . fear that no one will see me for who I am . . . fear that I'll be unnoticed like a breadcrumb on a table . . . and that I'll never be able to go back to my country and age like a palm tree, straight and uncurved. I fear that I won't be able to spend my last days in the water, like I used to when I was a child, when I lived in my bathing suit. Oh, I don't know why I always get the feeling that I'll forget how to swim.

BEMADETTE: Then go back to Colombia and swim.

LUCILA: Are you firing me?

BEMADETTE: Don't be ridiculous.

LUCILA: I can't recall whose idea it was for me to come to this
city when it's so cold. When I was in Cartagena I used to
spend the whole day in the water like a manatee.

BEMADETTE: Come, sit. Drink coffee with me.

(Lucila sits with Bemadette.)

LUCILA: You want me to read you your fortune on your coffee
cup?

BEMADETTE: What color are his eyes?

LUCILA: Brown.

BEMADETTE: What sort of brown?

LUCILA: Chestnut brown. He has puppy-dog eyes, sad and
innocent.

BEMADETTE: And his hands?

LUCILA: Like the hands of a poet.

BEMADETTE: Tell me, what's going on inside his head? Why is
he stalking an old woman like me?

LUCILA: He said he had come from far away, and I asked him
from how far. And he said it was not a matter of distance.
He was referring to all he had to go through before coming here.

BEMADETTE: You mean to get a visa and leave Cuba.

LUCILA: I guess.

BEMADETTE: But is he going to stay here?

LUCILA: No. He's here on a student visa. I only spoke to him
for a bit, and then I went to buy some olives.

BEMADETTE: With him?

LUCILA: No, by myself . . . for myself . . .

BEMADETTE: And why didn't you share your olives with him?

LUCILA: Because I prefer to eat olives privately and share
them with my solitude. That's why I eat them when I'm
alone at night.

28

(The phone rings. Bemadette answers. Lights reveal Saquiel. Lucila stays to listen to the conversation.)

SAQUIEL: Ms. Kahn, don't hang up. It doesn't matter if you don't talk to me. You don't have to tell me a word. —Ms. Kahn, are you there?

BEMADETTE: Yes.

SAQUIEL: Oh, I got a yes from you. We are making progress. Perhaps I can get another word from you.

BEMADETTE: I'm not mute . . .

SAQUIEL: I didn't think you were. When can I see you?

BEMADETTE: Why would a young man like you want to meet an old woman like me?

SAQUIEL: Don't worry. I won't be fresh.

BEMADETTE *(Laughs)*: Oh, I'm not worried. That didn't even cross my mind.

SAQUIEL: Then I should tell you that I prefer the wisdom of mature women than the naïveté of young women.

BEMADETTE: I sense you are asking me on a date. Are you asking me to go out, young man?

SAQUIEL: As a matter of fact, can I invite you to dinner?

BEMADETTE *(Playfully)*: Be careful Mr. Rafaeli. I might say yes, but I warn you I am not responsible for myself when I drink two martinis.

SAQUIEL: Then let me take you out.

BEMADETTE *(Laughs)*: Oh, I was just making fun of myself! But no, I don't go out.

(Lucila listens. She looks at Bemadette. She lowers her eyes.)

SAQUIEL: But it can still be a possibility, Ms. Kahn.

BEMADETTE: I beg your pardon.

SAQUIEL: We can still make it a reality.

BEMADETTE: I'm not sure I understand what you mean.

(It is difficult to know what Lucila is thinking, but she cannot bear the conversation. She rises to her feet and exits.)

SAQUIEL: We could meet without either one of us leaving the house.

BEMADETTE: And how is that possible, young man?

SAQUIEL: I'm referring to a virtual rendezvous through a computer screen.

BEMADETTE: A virtual rendezvous! I never heard of such a thing. It sounds a bit technological.

SAQUIEL: You'll see. We could just walk through the streets without walking on the streets. We could sit on park benches without actually sitting on them.

BEMADETTE: In that case we don't need a computer.

SAQUIEL: Are you saying you're open to my invitation?

BEMADETTE: Well, I'd much rather use my imagination and form a visual image of all the places we want to visit.

SAQUIEL: And where would you like me to take you?

BEMADETTE: You probably know the city better than I do.

SAQUIEL: I'm practically a foreigner here.

BEMADETTE: They're probably gone, all the places I used to visit.

SAQUIEL: Does it really matter if they're closed?

BEMADETTE: No. You're right.

SAQUIEL: Then take me to those places.

BEMADETTE *(Laughs)*: Now?

SAQUIEL: Why not?

BEMADETTE: In that case I must grab my purse to go out the door.

SAQUIEL: I'm already waiting for you downstairs.

BEMADETTE: I would have to powder my face.

SAQUIEL: In that case I should comb my hair.

BEMADETTE: I'll be ready in a second.

SAQUIEL: Then I will anticipate seeing you.

BEMADETTE: And what will you think about as you anticipate seeing me?

SAQUIEL: That my dear writer will look ravishing.

BEMADETTE: Yes. Like Nadine in my book. Young. Light on her feet. Wearing her silk dress, pearl earrings and a fedora hat.

SAQUIEL: Is it summer yet?

BEMADETTE: No, it would have to be spring if I wear my fedora hat.

SAQUIEL: Then I'll bring you flowers.

BEMADETTE: Tulips?

SAQUIEL: Red or Yellow?

BEMADETTE: No. Purple.

SAQUIEL: Purple then.

BEMADETTE: Young man, here I am!

(They look at each other through their imagination. The lights change to illustrate the virtual rendezvous.)

SAQUIEL: Ah, there you are! You look simply splendid.

BEMADETTE: Thank you. How-do-you-do, dear Student!

SAQUIEL: How-do-you-do, Ms. Kahn! I'm happy now that you're here.

BEMADETTE: Aren't you a gentleman!

SAQUIEL: I've been looking forward to seeing you.

BEMADETTE *(Steps out of the fantasy)*: I feel like such a fool doing this.

SAQUIEL: You mustn't judge yourself.

BEMADETTE: Never mind, I can fake it.

SAQUIEL: No, it should be real since you refuse to see me.

BEMADETTE: All right! Go on.

SAQUIEL: Well, now we just met. And I've kissed your hand.

BEMADETTE: In that case I will look at the sky and say, "My, I do hope the weather will keep good."

SAQUIEL: Then we walk and I tell you there's nowhere like New York in spring. —Should we go to Central Park?

BEMADETTE: I'd rather go to the Algonquin Hotel for some tea. Have you called a taxi?

SAQUIEL: I thought it would be better to hire a private chauffer. After all, I have a rendezvous with Ms. Bemadette Kahn.

(She laughs.)

BEMADETTE: Let's walk instead. It's not far from here.

SAQUIEL: Whatever you like, Ms. Kahn.

BEMADETTE: It's such a lovely day. How I miss walking through the city.

SAQUIEL: There's nothing like walking through Fifth Avenue and getting lost in a sea of people and stores.

BEMADETTE: Let's enter Saks Fifth Avenue.

SAQUIEL: Look, there's a lady asking you if you want to try on some perfume.

BEMADETTE: What kind?

SAQUIEL: I don't know. It looks expensive.

BEMADETTE: I only wear Molinard De Molinard and occasionally Shalimar.

SAQUIEL: Then it's Molinard. Can I buy you a bottle?

BEMADETTE *(Playfully)*: Young Student, when a man buys perfume for a lady it is expected that he'll want to smell it on her skin.

SAQUIEL: Ms. Kahn, you mustn't give me ideas that you'll later regret.

BEMADETTE *(Laughs)*: Well, in that case. *(As if singing)* Let's continue walking. Let's continue walking.

SAQUIEL: Let's walk over to Broadway where it never gets dark.

BEMADETTE: Is it night already?

SAQUIEL: Yes, and the theaters are about to open.

BEMADETTE *(Coquettish)*: Hum! Nighttime and me walking with a young man!

SAQUIEL: Holding hands . . .

BEMADETTE: I can't help feeling that this is impossible.

SAQUIEL: But are you happy?

BEMADETTE: Ecstatically!

SAQUIEL: That's all right then, isn't it?

BEMADETTE: Oh, it's perfect. Take me to see a play.

SAQUIEL: In Berlin, you couldn't be like this with Ariel Strauss.

BEMADETTE: In Berlin you couldn't do anything after 1933. I had many photos that showed me in Berlin with my friends, many who were Jewish. But after 1933 everything changed.

SAQUIEL: Where did you meet Ariel Strauss?

BEMADETTE: His father had a bookstore in Berlin. It was there that I discovered the books of Thomas Mann, Colette, Virginia Woolf . . .

SAQUIEL: And you discovered Ariel Strauss.

BEMADETTE: Yes and Ariel Strauss. But he wasn't a writer. He was an avid reader. *Gott* [God], I don't want to remember Berlin.

(The lights go back to normal.)

SAQUIEL: Why is that, Ms. Kahn?

BEMADETTE: Because for many years I wanted to forget that chapter in my life and what kills memory is not remembering. Why meet him again in a memory?

SAQUIEL: Perhaps to write about him.

BEMADETTE: I've never been able to write about Ariel Strauss.

SAQUIEL: You mentioned him in one of your books.

BEMADETTE: Yes I did. He was my first love. My Jewish lover from Berlin.

SAQUIEL: So there's nothing left for you to say about Ariel Strauss.

BEMADETTE: No.

SAQUIEL: And yet he's still there in your mind.

BEMADETTE: Yes. He's still there; the way things become frozen in time.

SAQUIEL: So you lack the courage?

BEMADETTE: Do you mean the courage to bring him to light?

SAQUIEL: Yes.

BEMADETTE: Maybe.

SAQUIEL: Is it that difficult for you to get rid of your feelings? I mean, by turning them into literature.

BEMADETTE: Some things can't be expressed through words. Becoming literature can never redeem what happened to Ariel Strauss and his sister Nina.

SAQUIEL: And yet history wants you to write about them.

BEMADETTE: No, not history. Only you.

SAQUIEL: Then he may already be in the book that you can't write.

BEMADETTE: I don't want it to be a revenge on life or for it to be on the side of melancholy.

SAQUIEL: I think whatever story you decide to write you're the only one who can write it.

BEMADETTE: Can we talk tomorrow?

SAQUIEL: No, you're not going yet! Don't go yet.

BEMADETTE: I'll expect your call tomorrow. Same time.

SAQUIEL: Ms. Kahn! Ms. Kahn.

(The lights fade.
We are at a dance studio. We hear the recorded voice of a dance instructor teaching the waltz. Lights reveal Lucila joining Saquiel in the initial dance position.)

VOICE OF DANCE INSTRUCTOR: Men will start with their left foot forward . . . Ladies will start with their right foot back . . . And one two three . . . and one two three . . . One more time, one two three . . . one two three . . .

(The couple dances to a waltz. Music plays: The Chopin Waltz in A minor, op. 69, no. 1. A blue sea is projected on

*the curtain. Bemadette enters, narrating the story that she
has begun writing.)*

BEMADETTE: Ariel and Nina Strauss never expected to be sailing on such a big and luxurious ship.
The brother and sister roamed around through the
decks, inspecting the lofty and ornate salons of the ocean
liner.

*(Although Lucila and Saquiel are dancing in the present,
they become Ariel and Nina Strauss in 1939. The lights
change to signify the shift of time.)*

ARIEL: The ship is moving! The ship is moving!
NINA: We're leaving! We're finally leaving!

(Bemadette turns to Ariel and Nina Strauss.)

BEMADETTE *(Almost in a whisper)*: Ariel . . . Nina . . . *(Waves
to them)* I will meet you in Havana! I will see you in
Havana! Write to me!
ARIEL: We'll be waiting for you!
NINA: I'll write to you soon!
BEMADETTE: There were families waving their hands and hand-
kerchiefs as the tugs towed the ship to the open sea. A band
was even playing music and flags were flying in the wind.
NINA: Feel the pure sea air . . . Good-bye, Germany! I see all
the things we're leaving behind. But we must close our
eyes and say to ourselves that they were never ours . . .
ARIEL: Of course they were. We're German . . . we're German . . .
we were born in Germany . . . Why are you saying that?
NINA: Because there are no more streets for us to walk through
in Germany . . . No more stores for us to shop in . . . No
concerts for us to attend . . .

BEMADETTE: Ariel and Nina Strauss thought there was someone important on the ship. They never found out who was the important passenger on board. But they felt special and later in the evening they pretended to be the guests of honor as they danced to a waltz.

ARIEL: Maybe we are indeed the guests of honor and that song is being played for us.

NINA *(Playfully)*: Monsieur, do you not recognize the music?

ARIEL: Yes, they're playing Chopin for us.

NINA: I haven't gone to the beauty shop in so long, I shall like to get my hair done.

ARIEL: Not so fast, little sister.

NINA: Why not, my porcupine?

ARIEL: We can't be spending our money in beauty salons.

NINA: Who says?

ARIEL: I do. I have the money.

NINA: Tomorrow I want to look divine at the ball . . .

ARIEL: We can't spend our savings.

NINA: In Cuba we'll work and make money.

ARIEL: Then in Cuba you can go to a beauty salon.

NINA: It's not a matter of vanity, Ariel.

ARIEL: Then what, little sister?

NINA: It's feeling the liberty of entering places we were banned from in our country and saying once again: "I'd like to get my hair cut like this woman in this magazine. Or I'd like to try this perfume."

ARIEL: All in due time, little sister. All in due time.

(He lifts her up in the air and swivels her. She shouts, full of joy.)

BEMADETTE: Night fell and the moon floated in the water like debris, like the ghost from a sunken ship.

My father had purchased the two tourist-class tickets at six hundred reichsmarks for Ariel and his sister. My father had been a good friend of their father. He thought it'd be best to send them to Cuba . . .

(Lights fade on Ariel and Nina Strauss.
Sound of the telephone ringing. The answering machine
picks up the call. Lights reveal Saquiel.)

SAQUIEL: Bemadette, are you there? It's Saquiel. Are you there?

(Bemadette picks up the phone.)

BEMADETTE: Yes, this is Bemadette.

SAQUIEL: I didn't think you would answer.

BEMADETTE: You never call at this time.

SAQUIEL: I've been trying to reach you for a few days.

BEMADETTE: I know. I've missed your voice.

SAQUIEL: Why didn't you answer the phone?

BEMADETTE: I was writing. What have you done to me? I'm writing again.

SAQUIEL: That's a good thing, isn't it?

BEMADETTE: Yes. Your voice. It's good to hear your gentle voice again.

SAQUIEL: I've started writing too. I'm writing about us.

BEMADETTE: What could you write about me?

SAQUIEL: I write about what I don't know about you. There can be no relation stranger than ours.

BEMADETTE: Is that because we've never met in person?

SAQUIEL: It is strange. After all, we're two people who only know each other through words and our voices.

BEMADETTE: Sometimes that's all that is needed.

SAQUIEL: Only the voice, Ms. Kahn?

BEMADETTE: Yes, only the voice. Don't call me Ms. Kahn anymore. Call me Bemadette. And I shall call you Ariel Strauss.

SAQUIEL: Why Ariel Strauss?

BEMADETTE: Because you have brought him back to me. And he has brought you to me. Because, for me, you are him. And it's frightening writing about you.

SAQUIEL: Why frightening?

BEMADETTE: To hear your voice, my Ariel Strauss, and to want to tell you what I'm writing about, as if you would understand.

SAQUIEL: I have understood everything else that you've written.

BEMADETTE: I could never resign myself to think that you were gone forever, my Ariel Strauss. I thought you and your sister Nina had only disappeared. That's what I was writing about this morning.

SAQUIEL: Do you have any idea what became of them?

BEMADETTE: They say the ship dropped anchor early on the morning of May 27 at the Havana harbor and was denied entry to the usual docking areas. The next six days in the harbor seemed endless. Then it was finally announced that the passengers would only be allowed to disembark if they had official Cuban visas.

SAQUIEL: And of course they didn't.

BEMADETTE: No, not Ariel and Nina. And neither did the other Jews. No one thought it was needed. Only twenty-two Jewish passengers were allowed to disembark on Cuban shores. After long negotiations, the remaining 908 Jewish passengers, would try their luck in Miami. But they met the merciless face of America, since entry was also denied to them.

SAQUIEL: Did you think this was a plan devised by the Nazis?

BEMADETTE: No, no one knew that at that time.

SAQUIEL: But the *St. Louis* was forced to return to Europe, showing the world that no one wanted the Jewish refugees.

BEMADETTE: Yes. And among those émigrés were Ariel and Nina.

SAQUIEL: Did you know what country they ended up in?

BEMADETTE: Much later.

SAQUIEL: And what country was that?

BEMADETTE: Belgium. But I lost touch with them.

SAQUIEL: They didn't write?

BEMADETTE: I don't know if they did. But I never got any letters. Much later I found out that they had been taken to a camp called Mechelen, halfway between Brussels and Antwerp.

SAQUIEL: When did you find out?

BEMADETTE: After the war. After it was all over.

SAQUIEL: And from there? From the camp?

BEMADETTE: I was told they were transported to another camp in the east, from where no one seemed to return.

SAQUIEL: The truth is that most passengers on that ship were sent to death camps.

BEMADETTE: But I didn't want to know that!

SAQUIEL: So you stopped your inquiry.

BEMADETTE: Yes! I stopped! I stopped! I didn't want to accept the truth of it all! For me, Ariel and Nina stayed on that ship bound for Cuba, where we were supposed to meet.

SAQUIEL: So you'd much rather remember Ariel and Nina alive . . .

BEMADETTE: Yes, yes . . . on their way to Cuba . . . before they were denied refuge in Havana and Miami.

SAQUIEL: But this journey became their end.

BEMADETTE: No, it was supposed to be their beginning.

SAQUIEL: Why is it so difficult for you to admit . . . ?

BEMADETTE: Admit what? What? That sending them back to Europe was the same as killing them?

SAQUIEL: That's a fact.

BEMADETTE: No. That's like letting darkness fall upon them or covering them with a wall of certainty.

SAQUIEL: That's what happened. Even God can't change what took place.

BEMADETTE: But I see so clearly what God could've prevented and how He should've intervened. I stopped praying after that.

(She looks into the distance.
Sound of foghorns and the cries of seagulls.)

It's that day of the crossing, when Ariel and Nina leave for Cuba, that I start loving Ariel with the same blind faith of a Jew. And it's with that same strength of faith that I confront my father. I ask him if he has bought tickets for Ariel and Nina on the *St. Louis* to get rid of them. My father tells me they're better off in Cuba—away from the madness, away from the chaos all around us, away from this hellish nightmare. "But away from me! Away from me!" I shout. "Yes, away from you," he tells me. "It couldn't go on," he says. "A Gentile and a Jew . . . it just couldn't go on, my little *Babs.* Not now, Bemadette . . . not now, *meine Liebling* [my darling]." —My father tells me he's done this to protect them, to protect me.

My father . . . my poor father . . . he thinks he's saving Ariel and Nina . . . he thinks he's offering me salvation. —From then on everything becomes a blur. I walk around the city and try to find myself in Berlin . . . But Berlin is no longer a place for me. I can't live here anymore. I stare at the puddles of rain evaporating on the streets and the memory of Ariel invades my body. Like the vanishing rain he begins to rise and become every part of my being. The memory of him pursues me everywhere. It emblazons me. A stare from a stranger, a glare from a passerby, a shaft of light, reminds me that he's within me, he has become part of my being, I have become my Jewish lover. I am Ariel Strauss, naked and defenseless. Even though I don't have a star pinned to my dress, my

star is there, invisible, fixed to my chest . . . because
I carry within me the memory of a Jew, a Jew who was my
beloved. So I too have become a Jew . . . A Jew in a city,
in a country that wants to exterminate all Jews.
SAQUIEL *(Gently)*: How old would Ariel Strauss be now?
BEMADETTE: He would be as old as I am and as young as you are.

(Suddenly, she smiles gently. Then, playfully:)

But are you trying to find out my age?
SAQUIEL: I know how old you are.
BEMADETTE *(Laughs)*: So my nineteen years did me in?
SAQUIEL *(Following her playfulness and sense of humor)*: Not
necessarily.
BEMADETTE: Ah, young man, if you only knew that in the
mathematic of age every wrinkle is counted.
SAQUIEL: And who counts?
BEMADETTE: Probably God, to remind us of our end.
SAQUIEL: Have you written all this down?
BEMADETTE: No. Another Bemadette who is foolish and mad
has written about it. Because to babble over scraps of life
is to betray the past.
SAQUIEL: You're not babbling, Bemadette . . .
BEMADETTE: I am. Memories are inefficient, and very impolite.
SAQUIEL: But they're also obedient to some extent.
BEMADETTE: And what good does divulging these memories
do, young man?
SAQUIEL: They're part of you! They're a part of who you are!
Trust your story. Trust me.
BEMADETTE: Believe me, my hands would love to hand you
every page, but my memories are unconvinced.
SAQUIEL: Then trust your hands.
BEMADETTE *(Smiles)*: You always say what I'd like to hear,
don't you?

SAQUIEL: I just say what comes to mind.

BEMADETTE *(Smiles and shakes her head in disbelief)*: I don't know what I'm going to do when you're gone.

SAQUIEL: I will come back.

BEMADETTE *(Laughs)*: If Lucila were eavesdropping on our conversation, she would think we're having an affair.

SAQUIEL: I think we are.

BEMADETTE: You think there's a love affair here?

SAQUIEL: Yes. If voices could have affairs that would be the case.

BEMADETTE: In fact, now that I think about it . . . There's more than one affair: writer and student, youth and old age. *(She laughs)*

SAQUIEL: You're laughing. How good to hear you laugh.

BEMADETTE: This is what happens when one lives with silence for so long, one runs the risk of falling for a voice.

(She laughs, coughs and becomes light-headed.)

Oh God, all of a sudden I feel very tired. As if . . .

SAQUIEL: Do you want to hang up?

BEMADETTE: No. I'm afraid.

SAQUIEL: Are you all right? *(Pause)* Bemadette.

BEMADETTE: Maybe I should hang up.

SAQUIEL: Can I call you later? Bemadette. Are you all right?

(All of a sudden Bemadette has a blank stare. She becomes very pale, as if life has abandoned her.)

Bemadette . . . Bemadette . . . Are you there . . . ? Bemadette . . . Are you all right?

    Bemadette . . . Bemadette.

(Bemadette is motionless, sitting in her chair.
Blackout. Music plays.)

Act Two

The lights reveal Saquiel and Lucila in Bemadette's apartment. Lucila has filled the apartment with votive candles.

LUCILA: She probably had a mild stroke—nothing that would affect her speech or coordination.

SAQUIEL: I kept calling the house to see how she was doing.

LUCILA: She'll be fine. Her Coumadin level was low. They have her on a new medication.

SAQUIEL: How is she feeling?

LUCILA: She's much better.

SAQUIEL: Will she let me see her when she's back from the hospital?

LUCILA: No. And now much less.

SAQUIEL: Why?

LUCILA: Vanity.

SAQUIEL: I'm not romancing the woman for God's sake!

LUCILA: It would be ridiculous if you were.

SAQUIEL: Do you have something against it?

LUCILA: Me? I could care less. I once wanted to fall in love with a blind man. I liked the fact that he couldn't see me but he could imagine me.

(Saquiel touches the walls. His hand glides over her books, her chair and every object on her desk. He sits on Bernadette's chair.)

SAQUIEL: Is this where she writes?

LUCILA: Don't touch anything. Leave everything in its place. She'll be discharged from the hospital tomorrow. She'd fire me if she ever found out that I brought you here.

(He inspects some of the objects on top of her desk.)

SAQUIEL: But everything is so personal, so beautiful.

LUCILA: You wouldn't find anything beautiful if you had to clean and dust like I do.

(He picks up an ashtray.)

SAQUIEL: Does she smoke?

LUCILA: Not allowed.

SAQUIEL: Did she use to?

LUCILA: Like a chimney.

SAQUIEL: Drink?

LUCILA: Like a desert.

SAQUIEL: Now?

LUCILA: She has wine.

(He sits in another chair.)

SAQUIEL: Does she like to sit in this chair?

LUCILA: Is it only Ms. Kahn that interests you?

SAQUIEL: No, of course not.

(He continues to explore everything in the house.)

LUCILA: I thought we could talk about other things.

SAQUIEL: Like what?

LUCILA: I don't know. Were you silent when you were a child? Did you live in a big house? What's it like living in Cuba? Do you cook? Do you like to play Parcheesi, Solitaire?

SAQUIEL: We can talk about that later. Can you show me her writing?

LUCILA: No. I can't do that.

SAQUIEL: Then why did you bring me here?

LUCILA: I thought you'd like to see the place where she lives.

SAQUIEL: Come on, show me!

LUCILA: Can't you take no for an answer?

SAQUIEL: She doesn't have to find out.

LUCILA: I said no! *(She moves away from him and goes for her purse)* Let's go now. Let's leave. This was a bad idea. I shouldn't have brought you here. *(She looks for her keys in her purse)*

SAQUIEL: All right! All right! Forget what I said. That was nothing what happened just now. Can we stay here for a bit longer?

(She walks to another part of the room.)

LUCILA: What would you do if I gave you the keys to this place?

SAQUIEL: I would try to find her writing and read it.

LUCILA: Why?

SAQUIEL: Because what's written is meant to be read, and books exist to help us understand ourselves.

LUCILA: What if I tell you that I have read some of her new writing? That I pieced together some papers she had thrown in the trash.

SAQUIEL: So you have saved all her mistakes.

LUCILA: Yes, you can say that I have. But I don't know if I saved them to understand her or myself . . . or even you . . .

SAQUIEL: Did you learn something from reading them?

LUCILA: I think I did.

SAQUIEL: What?

LUCILA: About intimate disaster. Pain.

SAQUIEL: What are you going to do with these papers?

LUCILA: Keep them for now.

SAQUIEL: Have you ever been tempted to sell them?

LUCILA: I think you're one step ahead of me.

SAQUIEL: What are they, notes?

LUCILA: Abandoned chapters.

SAQUIEL: Manuscripts that have mistakes are worth more than the ones that are polished.

LUCILA: Why is that?

SAQUIEL: Because you see the writer at work.

LUCILA: I wouldn't sell her writing. I'm not a person that goes for that sort of thing. I'm old-fashioned.

SAQUIEL: If you don't sell them, what will you do with them?

LUCILA: Probably donate them to a library when she's gone.

SAQUIEL: Or give them to me?

LUCILA (*Smiles with seduction*): Do you think you can persuade any woman to do anything?

SAQUIEL: No. But maybe you thought of me when you saved them from the trash.

LUCILA: Yes. I can say that I did.

SAQUIEL: You see. You're good to me.

(She turns away from him.)

LUCILA: There's no point in talking like that. I'm not going to give them to you.

SAQUIEL: Is there something I can learn from these papers?

(She turns to him. She looks at him, then with complete sincerity:)

LUCILA: What can you learn from a woman who had an encounter with a Nazi?

SAQUIEL *(Confused)*: You mean an affair?

LUCILA: Well, I wouldn't call it a romance.

SAQUIEL: Then what?

LUCILA *(Taking out a small stack of papers)*: Here. You can read it.

(He looks at her then he begins to read from the manuscript. Blue lights illuminate the stage. Bernadette enters.)

SAQUIEL: "The Nazi officer is barely nineteen years old. His gray-blue eyes are inclined to squint not only because they are extremely sensitive to the glare of light, but also because he wants to emphasize his manhood, and conceal his frailty."

(Bernadette continues to narrate the story as he reads in silence.)

BERNADETTE: Despite the military uniform and the gun that hangs from his belt, a strange attraction draws me towards this young soldier, a sensation unknown to me, indescribable, unforeseen—unnamable. The young officer looks at my neck and my bosom, as if he's never seen a woman before. I'm afraid of the dark feeling that assails me. There's something not quite right about my emotion, so precarious, so unbound and involuntary.

He is not the man who has killed my lover but he represents the enemy. He is a Nazi soldier and therefore he is the embodiment of the killer. Suddenly, my eyes turn to his gun. I see the unclasped holster. I lunge at him, grasp-

ing for his revolver; he instinctively shoves me away;
I leap at him yelling, "I want you to kill me—the same way
that my lover has been extinguished from life . . . You can
do with me as you want." I catch the soldier unguarded,
unprepared. I'm not part of his war. This is not what he's
expected to do as a soldier. For a moment desire had made
him forget the hatred, the violence, the purpose he was
fighting for. Now he feels pity for a woman who has lost her
lover in the war. The soldier wants to know my name. I tell
him, "I'm Ariel Strauss, a Jew from Berlin." This makes
his blood boil, the fact that he's attracted to a woman, a
Gentile, who has taken the identity of a Jew? He grabs
me by the arms, throws me to the floor and tears up my
clothes, with a brutality unknown to him. Then he stops.
He stops. He lies unmoving on top of my body, with the
weight of the dead, because he doesn't know what to do
with me. He doesn't know how to kill me. He's a soldier,
but he doesn't know how to end my life the way I want him
to. Slowly he pulls himself off of me and stands up from
the floor. "I won't kill you," he says. "I can't kill you." He
tells me he wanted to know me, to hold me, to discover
me. He wanted to know who I was, where I was born, and
what I love most in life. Then I realize he is also a victim
of war, and he wants to retain the right of judgment—to
understand my pain and for me to understand him—as a
man—and not as a servant of war. He cries. He can't stop
crying. "Go . . . !" he tells me. "Live! Please, live."

*(Bernadette exits. The lights go back to normal. Saquiel
and Lucila are stunned.)*

LUCILA: Do you understand her better now?
SAQUIEL *(As if he were elsewhere)*: It's not about understanding her.

LUCILA: Then what?

SAQUIEL: It's about recognizing her in us.

LUCILA: I can never recognize her in me or myself in her. I feel like a coward.

SAQUIEL: Why a coward?

LUCILA: Because I'm incapable of living to such an extent. After hearing you read, I feel I have no life left. As if she has lived it all for me. And I don't know . . . I'm suddenly afraid.

SAQUIEL: Afraid of what?

LUCILA: Of Bemadette . . . of you . . . of myself. *(With devastating frankness)* What's it like to love a woman without seeing her in person?

SAQUIEL *(Unprepared for this question, not knowing how to respond)*: I don't know. I . . . I imagine it would be like loving a soul . . .

LUCILA: No one has ever loved me like that. No one has ever taken interest in me without seeing me. I never liked my body or my face. I am uncomfortable with myself. I never thought that I was beautiful or interesting, and much less smart, the way that Ms. Kahn is intelligent. I lack grace. I feel awkward and clumsy, as if my blood is thin, and I have a hand-me-down heart. And yet I have never lost faith in loving and being loved invisibly.

(She turns and walks through the living room, trying to clothe the nakedness of her vulnerability. She begins to talk about Bemadette but she's actually talking about herself.)

—It will be difficult for Bemadette when you leave. It's because of you she's writing again.

SAQUIEL: I think she's writing the story she always wanted to write.

LUCILA: But that's what's kept her going. And the day she writes it all down, it might be all over for her.

SAQUIEL: Then she can write about how she got to write this book.

LUCILA: So the writing will never stop.

SAQUIEL: No. Never. What are you going to do with these papers?

LUCILA: I don't know.

SAQUIEL: I thought you would give them to me.

LUCILA: I thought so too. But no.

SAQUIEL: Why, because they're precious to you?

LUCILA: No, because they're private sorrows. And they will keep me company as I live my life.

SAQUIEL: And if one day you decide you can live without them?

LUCILA: I will give them to you.

SAQUIEL: Then I shall give you my address.

LUCILA: I'd much rather if you come back to get them in person, with the same purpose you came to visit Bernadette. But I'd have what you're looking for.

(He looks at her. She becomes nervous.)

I better close the windows.

(She goes to close the windows. He stops her.)

SAQUIEL: No, leave them open.

(She looks at him with fear.)

LUCILA: Did you like coming here today?

SAQUIEL: Yes.

LUCILA: Let's go to the dining room. We can see sundown from there.

SAQUIEL: Let's spend the night here.

(She doesn't answer. She starts walking, then she turns to him.)

LUCILA: There's less light there. And you won't have to see me.

(He turns to her.)

SAQUIEL: But I want to look at you.

(She lowers her head and walks out. The lights fade to black.
We hear the sound of the computer chime. Lights up on Bemadette, sending an email to Saquiel.)

BEMADETTE: Dear Student, I'm feeling well this morning and I'm writing again. Today I wept like a child knowing you are leaving. Send.

(Lights up on Saquiel.)

SAQUIEL: Dear Writer, if the *St. Louis* conference is held back here in the States this September, I will be able to return. Send.

BEMADETTE: Dear Student, when you come back from Havana, please carry back with you all of my letters from the *St. Louis*. Send.

SAQUIEL: Dear Writer, today is such a fine day for us to go on an outing.

BEMADETTE: Dear Student, should I get my purse and have our final rendezvous?

SAQUIEL: As long as you feel young and strong in feeling that's what matters.

BEMADETTE: You have cured me, my clever young man. What I beg of you, hope for, long for, is for you to trust our invisibility. It is something like faith, devoted to the unseen.

SAQUIEL: I have the photograph you sent me of when you were young.

BEMADETTE *(Laughs at herself)*: Do I look beautiful?

SAQUIEL *(Smiles)*: Very beautiful. Stunning. *(Absolute truth)* In the evening I met your ghost in the streets.

BEMADETTE: And how did I look?

SAQUIEL *(Smiles)*: You looked sensual, like your photographs.

BEMADETTE *(Innocently surprised)*: I did?

SAQUIEL: Yes. You had a silk dress.

BEMADETTE *(Lost in a reverie)*: And was I young again? I mean, my ghost?

SAQUIEL *(In the present)*: You were.

BEMADETTE *(Delicately)*: You can tell me the truth this time. Another young woman resembling me, you mean?

SAQUIEL *(Full of sincerity)*: Yes. I met her at . . . I met her on the street. She had your eyes.

BEMADETTE *(Remembering what her own eyes looked like)*: My eyes?

SAQUIEL: Yes, your eyes.

BEMADETTE *(Remembering desire on her lips, rediscovering it)*: My lips?

SAQUIEL: Yes, your lips. Your neck.

BEMADETTE: My neck. *(Caressing her neck)* My hair?

SAQUIEL: Yes, your hair. Your breasts. Your hips. Your legs.

BEMADETTE *(Remembering her youth)*: She was young. And you had her in your arms.

SAQUIEL: Yes.

BEMADETTE *(Smiles, lost in memory)*: My! To be young again . . . ! To be young and naive . . . Oh, la, la! I would have to be more cautious by this candor if I were dealing with an ordinary young man, but you are not ordinary. You are eccentric like me.

SAQUIEL: I'll never forget you, Bemadette, whatever happens.

BEMADETTE: Oh, your voice, Saquiel.

SAQUIEL: I will call you from the airport to say good-bye.

BEMADETTE *(Almost exhausted)*: No. Do not call me, I prefer a little silence today while I try to get used to your absence.

(The lights fade on Saquiel.
Bemadette presses a button on the answering machine to retrieve a message. We hear the voice of Saquiel. Bemadette listens to Saquiel's message.)

SAQUIEL *(Recorded voice)*: Bemadette, are you there? It's me. —I don't think you will answer the phone. But let me tell you my plans. My grandfather will lend all his documents for the conference in Miami. I plan to create an exhibition with more than two hundred documents and pictures of the *St. Louis* passengers. I will read two papers: "*St. Louis*, the ship of indifference" and "Bemadette, or the memory of disquiet." All documents must be ready by the 4th of September. I hope you send me your pages about Ariel and Nina Strauss.

(The lights reveal Saquiel.)

(Spoken voice) Bemadette? —I know you won't answer. My plans are to be back to New York after the convention. Even with the pathetic amount I earn for my work at the library and a little money my aunt sends from Miami, I think I'll be able to save enough to visit you for a month. —Bemadette, are you listening? I promise I'll come back. I have basically lived out of my backpack for the last two months. The woman who lets me stay at her house told me

I could come back and stay with her. I contribute a little by washing her dishes, doing her laundry and cleaning her house. She's quite lonely so she likes my company and she lets me sleep on her sofa. *(With a warm smile)* If I can't stay with her, I can stay with someone else. I'm not worried about that. New York is full of people who rent out their couches, their closets, their kitchens . . . I know an artist who rents a window from a retired librarian. —Can you believe it? It's a big window with lots of light and a good view of the river, so he goes there and paints in front of the window. There's another man who rents out his dining table, so you can use the top of the table for writing and the space underneath for sleeping. I'll keep this in mind as another option. And there's another man who rents out his bathtub if you want to take a bath or sleep in the bathtub. Sometimes you don't have to pay these people anything. You can negotiate a deal like walking their dogs or cooking for them. Either way, I'll find a place for myself in New York.

Bemadette! *(Slight pause)* All right, I'm going to go now. My flight's boarding. I'll call you from *la Habana*. *(In despair)* —I know you don't want to say good-bye, but at least wish me a safe trip.

(He is shattered. Lights fade down on Saquiel. He's gone. She stays without moving.)

BEMADETTE *(In a soft voice, toward the distance)*: Be well.

(She sits in a chair. The lights fade down and then back up, to illustrate the passage of time.
Bemadette remains sitting in the chair throughout the following sequence. Soft music plays. Lights up on Lucila.)

LUCILA: Late June 2000. Dear Saquiel, I'd have just received your postcard. I feel I want to become something other than a woman who waits for your return. I'd much rather be a wave or an ivy that can travel in your direction. Waiting is unbearable, even when you know why you wait. I eat olives and think of your mouth. I eat chocolate and imagine kissing your eyebrows. I hope I don't gain too much weight by the time you come back.

BEMADETTE: Early July 2000. Dear Student, my sotto voce, I suppose one shouldn't be writing letters like this at my age. But I still wonder at my good fortune, how this blind enchantment so late in my life has taken me from the distrustful soul I was to an almost adolescent girl, infatuated with life all over again. It would have been far easier to keep my memories buried. I have finally comprehended what it means to remember. The only thing that worries me is Lucila. What did you do this young woman, Mr. Rafaeli?

(Lights up on Saquiel.)

SAQUIEL: Mid-July 2000. Dear Lucila, I am tirelessly preparing for my trip to the States. Forgive the lightness of my writing, I only have one pen and it is running out of ink. I miss you, my porcupine.

LUCILA: Late July 2000. Dear Saquiel, I'm afraid this is a silly letter. I wish I had literary aspirations and I wasn't a housemaid who has to continue making beds, washing dishes and sweeping floors. But I'd do anything to serve you and for you to be happy, for nothing has changed in my love for you.

BEMADETTE: Dear Student, my sotto voce, how is it with you? The flat is full of the smell of another lamb stew Lucila is making. By the way, her birthday is on the eighteenth.

When September brings you, we will skip autumn and winter, and return to our spring together.

SAQUIEL: Early August 2000. Dear Bemadette, it's better after all that you and Lucila didn't receive my past two letters. They were very unhappy in every sense of the word. The government of Cuba is making it impossible for me to travel to the States. And the U.S. government is not allowing me to enter the country since I overextended my stay there.

(Bemadette stops reading the letter; she is quite dismayed. Lucila comes in with a tray. Lights fade down on Saquiel.)

LUCILA: Coffee, Ms. Kahn?

BEMADETTE: Please.

LUCILA: No writing today?

BEMADETTE: No, no writing.

LUCILA: It's been months now.

BEMADETTE: There are dry periods.

LUCILA: Then let it rain so you can finish!

BEMADETTE: Writing should never be about duty and work. You postpone, until the writing begins to promise pleasure again.

LUCILA: Then how do you finish anything?

BEMADETTE: Sit down and drink coffee with me.

(Lucila serves herself a cup of coffee.)

I just read a letter that Saquiel sent to me. He's not coming to the States. He's not coming back.

LUCILA: That can't be, Ms. Kahn.

BEMADETTE: Yes. The Cuban government is making it difficult for him to come back. And the U.S. government is not allowing him to enter the country because he overextended his stay.

LUCILA: Ay, Ms. Kahn, please don't tell me that.

BEMADETTE: I just wish there was a way of calling him on the phone.

LUCILA: So what's going to happen now?

BEMADETTE: I don't know. We'll have to wait until he calls from his neighbor's house.

LUCILA: Maybe you can write the Cuban consulate.

BEMADETTE: I'm not sure that would help.

LUCILA: You can make a case for him, Ms. Kahn. Wasn't he doing research? Didn't he come here to interview you?

BEMADETTE: Yes, but . . .

LUCILA: God, you have to do something!

BEMADETTE: And what can I do?!!

LUCILA: Help him get out! Help him come here! It's because of you he overextended his stay.

BEMADETTE: For God's sake, don't make me feel guilty!

LUCILA: It's the truth! It took him forever to find you. Then when he discovered where you lived you wouldn't meet with him. You didn't want to see him. That's why he had to stay longer.

BEMADETTE: It's destroying me . . . all of this . . .

LUCILA: It's reality, Ms. Kahn. I would help him if I could. It might sound silly but I would go to Cuba and marry him to get him out, but I can't do anything for him. It's impossible. I can't go there. I can never leave this country. I'm afraid I won't be allowed to come back. And as much as I love Colombia, I don't want to go back there. I don't want to live there. Not the way things are in my country.

BEMADETTE *(Full of sadness)*: I can't believe how this is happening again. And I was hoping, he and you . . .

LUCILA *(Trying to console her)*: Let's see what happens, Ms. Kahn.

BEMADETTE: God! How are we going to spend our days now?

LUCILA: The way we did before.

57

BEMADETTE: No. It won't be the same. It's difficult for me in the evenings . . . around sunset . . . I can't bear the stillness that follows when you close the door behind you. The muteness. The silence changes from the silence at dawn, from the silence at day and the silence at dusk. And it's not the quiet that might appease or soothe and numb the moment. This quietude has no future because it doesn't move forward or ahead. *(Suddenly an abstract idea)* I think I should go . . . I should go to Cuba.

LUCILA: You? I don't remember the last time you stepped out of this house.

BEMADETTE: I'm going to Havana and that's all there's to it.

LUCILA: I can't go with you.

BEMADETTE: Then I'll have to go by myself. It was always meant for me to go to Cuba. I was supposed to meet up with Ariel, back in my youth. Now it's time.

LUCILA: The government will make it difficult for you.

BEMADETTE: Nothing's going to stop me this time! No one will get in my way! I'll go and no law is going to stop me!

LUCILA: Finish drinking your coffee. I'm going to read your fortune. We'll see what your coffee grinds have to say about all this.

BEMADETTE: What are you talking about? What am I supposed to do?

LUCILA: Just finish sipping your coffee in a contemplative manner as you always do. I learned this from a Turkish friend.

(Bemadette sips her coffee.)

BEMADETTE: Now you're making me feel self-conscious.

LUCILA: Just enjoy your coffee then ask yourself: "What do I need to know about myself?"

BEMADETTE: All right, I'm done.

(Lucila covers the cup of coffee with the saucer and shakes it.)

LUCILA: It is said that the state of mind of the coffee-drinker affects the marks and forms that coffee leaves behind in the cup. And that's all it takes to read your fortune in your own cup of coffee.

(Lucila turns the cup upside down into the saucer. She takes the cup and starts scrying clockwise until she finishes back at the cup handle.)

The form of a fish left by the foam could signify money; the shape of a camel could mean that you are going to travel; a moon could symbolize romance in your life. The shape of a knife could hold clues that a man is coming your way.

(Bemadette laughs.)

BEMADETTE: I never knew that a cup of coffee could contain a drop of wisdom.

LUCILA: Hum! I see a cat.

BEMADETTE: A cat and not a fish? Is that bad luck?

LUCILA: No. The cat could be you.

BEMADETTE: Goodness! I never saw myself as a cat.

LUCILA: The cat has a sea wave in its mouth.

BEMADETTE: And what could that possibly mean?

LUCILA: The sea wave could be desire.

BEMADETTE: Desire?

LUCILA: If he's drinking the wave . . .

BEMADETTE: Is he drinking it?

LUCILA: Yes, like milk.

BEMADETTE: Then he's a naughty cat.

LUCILA: Here's a camel. That means travel.

BEMADETTE: How glad to know that a camel visits my cup.

LUCILA: Here's the form of a snake. That means health. You will have to be healthy enough to travel.

BEMADETTE: I will eat everything you cook for me.

LUCILA: Here's a turtle. Caution. You won't regret this trip, but you'll have to remain calm and rest.

BEMADETTE: How happy this trip makes me.

LUCILA: Please tell Saquiel why I won't go with you to see him.

(Lucila rises to her feet and leaves. Slowly, a seascape is projected on the curtain. Soft music begins to play. Bemadette rises to her feet and looks into the distance.)

BEMADETTE: I am already traveling. By the time I get to the island the sea waves will have advanced across the ocean and they will humble themselves when they reach the shore.

Some birds will think I am a dream. The port will think I am a ghost. A turtle will think I have only come to see and take the island with me. The snail will suspect that I've come in search of a home. But I'll have an existence of my own when I see Ariel Strauss.

(Now, the past, what could have been, merges with an inexplicable present. Saquiel appears dressed as Ariel Strauss. He wears a black raincoat and a fedora hat and is holding a suitcase. He calls out to Bemadette. She steps into this other dimension where anything is possible.)

I see you at the port coming towards me. Ah, to see you once again. Nothing has disturbed the waiting. Oh, you amazing, painfully lost, painfully innocent love!

How your presence endures. Nothing has disturbed the waiting.

END OF PLAY

Nilo Cruz is a Cuban-American playwright whose work has been produced widely across the U.S., including performances with such distinguished companies as Princeton's McCarter Theatre, New York's Public Theater and Manhattan Theatre Club. Internationally, Cruz's plays have been produced in Canada, England, France, Australia, Germany, Belarus, Costa Rica, Colombia, Panama, Ecuador, Japan, Russia, and in cities throughout Spain. In 2003, Cruz became the first Latino to win the Pulitzer Prize for Drama, thanks to his most celebrated work, *Anna in the Tropics*.